Nathanael Greene

Military Leader

Colonial Leaders

Lord Baltimore
English Politician and Colonist

Benjamin Banneker
American Mathematician and Astronomer

Sir William Berkeley
Governor of Virginia

William Bradford
Governor of Plymouth Colony

Jonathan Edwards
Colonial Religious Leader

Benjamin Franklin
American Statesman, Scientist, and Writer

Anne Hutchinson
Religious Leader

Cotton Mather
Author, Clergyman, and Scholar

Increase Mather
Clergyman and Scholar

James Oglethorpe
Humanitarian and Soldier

William Penn
Founder of Democracy

Sir Walter Raleigh
English Explorer and Author

Caesar Rodney
American Patriot

John Smith
English Explorer and Colonist

Miles Standish
Plymouth Colony Leader

Peter Stuyvesant
Dutch Military Leader

George Whitefield
Clergyman and Scholar

Roger Williams
Founder of Rhode Island

John Winthrop
Politician and Statesman

John Peter Zenger
Free Press Advocate

Revolutionary War Leaders

John Adams
Second U.S. President

Ethan Allen
Revolutionary Hero

Benedict Arnold
Traitor to the Cause

King George III
English Monarch

Nathanael Greene
Military Leader

Nathan Hale
Revolutionary Hero

Alexander Hamilton
First U.S. Secretary of the Treasury

John Hancock
President of the Continental Congress

Patrick Henry
American Statesman and Speaker

John Jay
First Chief Justice of the Supreme Court

Thomas Jefferson
Author of the Declaration of Independence

John Paul Jones
Father of the U.S. Navy

Lafayette
French Freedom Fighter

James Madison
Father of the Constitution

Francis Marion
The Swamp Fox

James Monroe
American Statesman

Thomas Paine
Political Writer

Paul Revere
American Patriot

Betsy Ross
American Patriot

George Washington
First U.S. President

Famous Figures of the Civil War Era

Jefferson Davis
Confederate President

Frederick Douglass
Abolitionist and Author

Ulysses S. Grant
Military Leader and President

Stonewall Jackson
Confederate General

Robert E. Lee
Confederate General

Abraham Lincoln
Civil War President

William Sherman
Union General

Harriet Beecher Stowe
Author of Uncle Tom's Cabin

Sojourner Truth
Abolitionist, Suffragist, and Preacher

Harriet Tubman
Leader of the Underground Railroad

Nathanael Greene

Military Leader

Meg Greene

Arthur M. Schlesinger, jr.
Senior Consulting Editor

Chelsea House Publishers

Philadelphia

Produced by 21st Century Publishing and Communications, Inc. New York, NY. http://www.21cpc.com

CHELSEA HOUSE PUBLISHERS
Production Manager Pamela Loos
Art Director Sara Davis
Director of Photography Judy L. Hasday
Managing Editor James D. Gallagher
Senior Production Editor J. Christopher Higgins

Staff for *NATHANAEL GREENE*
Project Editor/Publishing Coordinator Jim McAvoy
Project Editor Anne Hill
Associate Art Director Takeshi Takahashi
Series Design Keith Trego

The Chelsea House World Wide Web address is
http://www.chelseahouse.com

First Printing
1 3 5 7 9 8 6 4 2

Library of Congress Cataloging-in-Publication Data

Greene, Meg.
Nathanael Greene / Meg Greene.
   p. cm. — (Revolutionary War leaders)
Includes bibliographical references (p.) and index.
ISBN 0-7910-5977-4 (hc) — 0-7910-6135-3 (pbk.)
1. Greene, Nathanael, 1742–1786—Juvenile literature. 2. Generals—United States—Biography—Juvenile literature. 3. United States. Continental Army—Biography—Juvenile literature. 4. Quakers—United States—Biography—Juvenile literature. 5. United States—History—Revolution, 1775–1783—Juvenile literature. [1. Greene, Nathanael, 1742–1786. 2. Generals. 3. Quakers. 4. United States—History—Revolution, 1775–1783.] I. Title. II. Series.

E207.G9 G84 2000
973.3'3'092—dc21
[B]   00-038396
                                                                          CIP

Contents

Nathanael Greene's father was an ironsmith, like the one pictured here. As a boy, Nathanael worked hard in his father's ironworks and mill.

The Ironsmith's Son

Nathanael Greene was a cheerful and spirited boy. He liked roaming through the hills that rose around his hometown of Potowomut, Rhode Island. When necessary, he was glad to stop playing long enough to help his father with his work or one of his many brothers with their chores. Nathanael's playmates always found him ready to make them laugh with a joke. Among his Potowomut neighbors, young Nathanael quickly earned a reputation for generosity and kindness.

Nathanael was born on July 27, 1742, and was named after his father. His mother was Mary Mott

Greene. Not long after his birth, an **astrologer** told his parents that their new son would be "a great man." Both of his parents were **descendants** of prosperous **Quaker** families that had come to live in Rhode Island almost a century earlier.

Nathanael's **ancestors** arrived from England in 1635, ready to make a new life for themselves in the North American colonies. Arriving first in Massachusetts, the Greenes soon moved to the new colony of Rhode Island, where they could practice their Quaker faith without fear of **persecution**. Settling in Potowomut, which later became part of the town of Warwick, the Greenes soon established themselves as the successful owners of several **grist** and lumber mills. Later Nathanael's father also bought an iron **foundry**. There he made, among other things, anchors for the many ships that docked at Newport, Rhode Island. Newport was among the busiest ports along the eastern seaboard.

As a young boy, Nathanael learned to work

the **bellows** and keep track of supplies for the foundry, the mill, the family's barn, and his mother's kitchen. He also traveled with his father and his older brother Tom to the nearby towns of Warwick and Newport to buy, sell, and trade goods.

Nathanael worked very hard and took the responsibilities his father gave him seriously. Despite suffering from a bad knee that caused him to walk with a limp, Nathanael managed to keep up with his brothers and friends. Whether it was swinging the heavy sledgehammer at the **forge** or wrestling and racing across the countryside, Nathanael never let his disability slow him down. No one in Nathanael's family knew what caused the limp, but Nathanael was determined never to let the affliction get the better of him.

Nathanael loved to joke, whistle a tune, and have a good time. Despite long days of hard labor, he was always more than ready to have fun whenever an opportunity presented itself, even if it meant breaking the family curfew and

Boys playing crack-the-whip. Nathanael was always ready to play with his friends and go on nighttime adventures.

sneaking out of the house at night after he was supposed to be in bed. Nathanael would climb from his bedroom window onto the limbs of a nearby tree. Then he would shimmy down the trunk and set off into the night to do any number of things, such as going to a dance or a **husking bee**. Neighbors would shake their heads when they heard of the latest trouble that young

Nathanael had gotten himself into. But Nathanael always took whatever punishment his father and mother imposed without protest or complaint, regarding it as the price to be paid for his adventures.

While Nathanael's father wondered about the flaw in his son's character that drew him to such antics, there was another aspect of Nathanael's personality that disturbed him even more deeply. During the winter when work was slow, Mr. Greene hired a traveling tutor who stayed at the family home and taught Nathanael and his brothers how to read, write, and solve simple arithmetic problems. Mr. Greene was a devout Quaker and he believed that all a person

The Greene family was by no means living in poverty, but there was little extra money to buy the books that Nathanael loved so much. One story tells how Nathanael, in an attempt to raise money for books, started making small iron toys while at work at his father's foundry. On his trips to Newport and Warwick, he sold his toys to local storekeepers, or even bartered them in exchange for books! These efforts marked the beginning of Nathanael's dedication to building a personal library.

really needed to know was how to write his or her name, read the Bible, and keep business accounts in order. Nathanael's brothers felt the same way, so reading was not very important to them.

But Nathanael was different. Instead of seeing education as a necessary evil, or a way to pass the time during the inactivity of winter, Nathanael read every book he could lay his hands on and was eager to learn as much as he could. Nathanael's father considered this love of books another weakness in his son's character and tried to discourage Nathanael. These efforts failed miserably. In 1756, at the age of 14, Nathanael asked to go to a regular school.

As much as his father wanted to refuse his son's request, he could not bring himself to do so. Finally, he permitted Nathanael to attend the local school in East Greenwich, a small village not far from Potowomut. There, under the watchful eye of his teacher, a young Scot named Adam Maxwell, Nathanael was introduced to the world of learning.

Nathanael proved an excellent student. He

This is a page from the *New-England Primer*, the only grade school textbook in the New England colonies for 50 years. Nathanael loved to read when he was growing up.

displayed a quick, orderly mind to match his ready wit and showed a natural skill for mathematics. He also excelled in Latin and the classics.

Nathanael found his studies so enjoyable and became so determined to get an education that he often tended to his duties at the forge or the mill with a book in one hand, his finger marking the place at which he had left off reading. In the evenings when the family gathered at home around a roaring fire, he often excused himself and went upstairs to his bedroom, where he had built a tiny shelf for his books. There, by the flickering light of a candle, bundled in a warm blanket, he read for hours and hours, until he finally fell asleep.

As a young man, one of Nathanael's favorite activities was dancing; what he lacked in grace, he made up for in enthusiasm. One of his dancing partners once told him, "You dance stiffly, Nathanael." Nathanael took the comment lightly and replied with a laugh, "Very true, my dear, but you see that I dance strong."

For all his efforts, Nathanael was never satisfied with his progress. Throughout his life, he regretted his lack of formal schooling, once writing that "early, very early, when I should have been in the pursuit of Knowledge, I was digging into the

Bowels of the Earth after Wealth."

Not every aspect of Nathanael's life was as happy as the hours he passed with his books. During the winter of 1753, three years before he entered the academy at East Greenwich, Nathanael's mother died. Nathanael loved his mother dearly and took her death very hard.

As he grew older, Nathanael began thinking about his future. What would he do? Surely he and his half brother Thomas would one day take over the family business and continue what his ancestors had begun. The rest of his life must have seemed comfortably predictable. Nathanael could never have guessed that events were already underway that would change his life forever.

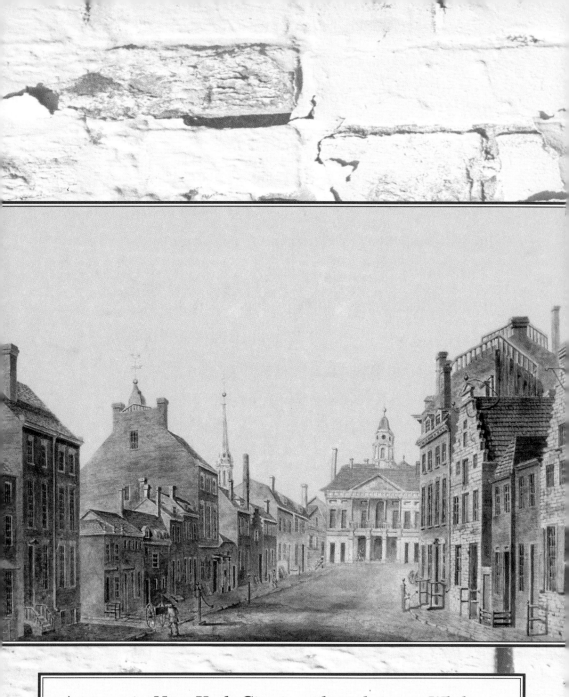

A street in New York City in colonial times. While studying law, Nathanael visited New York and other important American cities.

"Put from Under"

In 1760 Nathanael's passion for learning was called on to solve a family problem. His half brothers, Benjamin and Thomas, had recently died, and a there was a dispute over who should receive their inheritance. The family turned to Nathanael, with his ability to read and write, to sort out the legal business.

The lawsuit was eventually decided in favor of Nathanael, his father, and his surviving brothers. But Nathanael's reading of the law also offered him new experiences. While gathering evidence, he met lawyers, judges, and court clerks, not only in Rhode

Island but also in the neighboring colonies of Connecticut and New York. On one of his trips to New York, Nathanael was inoculated against the deadly disease of smallpox. The inoculation caused a fever that left him with a slight blemish in his right eye. Although the spot would sometimes become painful, Nathanael never regretted his decision to be vaccinated.

Nathanael Greene Sr. died in 1769. The next year, at the age of 28, Nathanael, along with his five brothers, took over the management of the family forge and gristmill in Coventry. Not long afterward, he built himself a comfortable eight-room house. Although the house reminded Nathanael of his boyhood home, it had something the other did not: a library. Here, at last, he could store his growing collection of books.

Even with his busy days at the forge and mill, Nathanael was restless. He soon found himself becoming more interested in local affairs. He wanted to do something to improve his hometown. Meeting with local officials, Nathanael

Men reading and talking in a tavern. Politics was always a topic of discussion in the months before the Revolutionary War broke out.

recommended that they form a public school system for Coventry. At first many resisted the idea. But in time, Nathanael won over the opponents of his idea. Thanks to his efforts, Coventry had its first public school and teacher.

A year later, in 1771, Nathanael was selected to be a deputy to the Rhode Island General Assembly. He served in that office through 1772, and then again in 1775. During that time, he acquired a reputation for his writing. Many of his colleagues envied his ability to study a problem and then clearly write his findings.

Nathanael still found time to relax even with his business and political responsibilities. In 1773, while attending a dance in East Greenwich, Nathanael met Catherine Littlefield. "Kitty," as she was known, was only 19 and an orphan. Nathanael was enchanted with her, and in 1774 the two were married. Nathanael returned to Coventry with his bride, where they led a quiet and happy life.

While Nathanael was busy courting Kitty and tending to his duties, other concerns were beginning to occupy the minds of many men in the British colonies. For more than 50 years, the colonists in America had been taxing themselves through their colonial legislatures. In 1764, the British government, with a huge war debt from fighting the French, decided it was time for the colonists to pay more taxes.

To protest the British tax on tea, some outraged colonists disguised themselves as Native Americans, boarded British ships, and threw the tea into the sea.

The colonists were not eager to pay them. More and more, the slogan "no taxation without representation" echoed from the crowded streets of Boston to the scattered farms of Virginia.

Colonists grew angry at the attempts of King George III and the British Parliament to control them. On the night of December 16, 1773, a number of colonists, dressed up as American Indians, snuck aboard a British ship in Boston Harbor, and threw the ship's entire cargo of tea into the icy waters to protest the new tax on tea.

Nathanael was excited to learn of the growing resistance against the king and Parliament. He was an early champion of independence and was among the first Rhode Islanders to openly stand up for freedom from Britain. An earlier incident in 1772 had ensured that Nathanael would not stand alone for long.

In June 1772, the *Gaspée,* a British vessel, chased an American ship suspected of smuggling. During the chase, the *Gaspée* ran ashore near Pawtucket, Rhode Island. A group of angry colonists, fed up with the British treatment of American ships, boarded the *Gaspée* and put the captain and crew ashore. They then set fire to the British ship.

Fire onboard a sailing ship. Angry Rhode Island colonists set fire to the *Gaspée*, a British vessel that ran aground while chasing an American ship.

British officials were furious and offered huge rewards for information leading to the arrest of the **culprits**. No informant stepped forward. A court of inquiry was held, and during the investigation Nathanael was named as one of the leaders of the group that had stormed and burned the ship. There was no evidence to prove his guilt, and Nathanael was outraged. He promised if he ever discovered the identity of his accuser, he would "put a hole in him big enough to let the sun shine through." The incident persuaded many of Nathanael's fellow Rhode Islanders to support American independence.

Shortly after the *Gaspée* affair, Nathanael met Henry Knox, a Boston bookseller. Nathanael looked forward to visiting Knox whenever he went to Boston on business. Together they discussed the politics of the day. Knox advised Nathanael on what books to buy for his library. It was at this time that Nathanael began reading military history and studying the **campaigns** of Caesar and Hannibal. Through Knox, Nathanael also got to know Samuel Adams, a lawyer, and Paul Revere, a silversmith.

Nathanael's new interest in military history,

combined with his growing sense that there might be war between the colonies and the **mother country**, brought him to a turning point in his life. As a Quaker, Nathanael had been raised a pacifist. A **pacifist**, or lover of peace, does not support war under any circumstances. If Nathanael joined the war effort against Great Britain, he would be cast out of Quaker society.

Nathanael did not have to wrestle long with this **dilemma**. One Sunday afternoon in June 1774, not long before he married Kitty, Nathanael and his cousin attended a military rally and exhibition in the nearby village of Plainfield, Connecticut. Nathanael could not conceal his excitement as he watched the **militia** units marching and drilling.

But when he returned home trouble awaited him. News of his activities had already reached the Quaker community of East Greenwich, where he and his family worshiped. A special committee evaluated Nathanael's conduct and sadly reported that since Nathanael had "not given this Meeting any satisfaction for [his] outgoing and misconduct . . . this Meeting doth put [him] from under the care of the Meeting." Nathanael was **banished** from the Quaker community.

The Quakers had settled the matter for him, and Nathanael never looked back. Instead, he immediately applied for membership in a volunteer militia known as the Kentish Guards of East Greenwich. Several of Nathanael's friends, who were also members of the company, argued that he ought to be considered for the rank of lieutenant instead of private. Others in the unit, though, decided they did not want anyone with a handicap to march with the Kentish Guards. They saw to it that Nathanael's application was rejected.

Nathanael was stunned. Never before had his handicap been used against him. His friends were similarly outraged. A boyhood friend, James Varnum, now an officer with the Guards, threatened to resign his commission if the unit did not accept Nathanael.

Although disappointed, Nathanael pleaded

with Varnum not to resign. "Let me **entreat** you, sir," Nathanael wrote, "if you have any regard for me, not to forsake the company at this critical season, for I fear the consequences. I would not have the company break and disband. . . . It would be a disgrace to the country."

Despite Nathanael's sincere requests, his friends continued to fight for him. At last, his opponents gave in and permitted Nathanael to join the Kentish Guards, but with the rank of private. After Nathanael paraded with his **musket**, no one said anything else about his limp. Little did anyone realize that in less than one year they would all be addressing lowly Private Greene as "general."

Nathanael may have at last been accepted into the Kentish Guards, but to stay in he needed a musket. But the British strictly prohibited the transport and selling of guns in the colonies. Despite the danger, Nathanael traveled to Boston, where he bought a musket. To carry the weapon home, he hid it in a local farmer's wagon, under the hay.

He also brought something else home from Boston for the Kentish Guards: a deserter from the British Army whom he had persuaded to act as drill master for the unit.

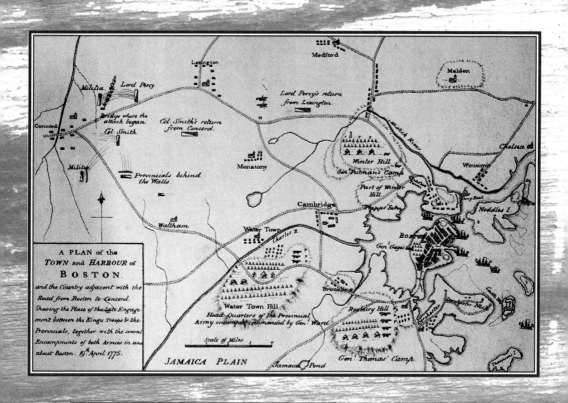

A map of Boston and the nearby towns of Lexington and Concord (upper left). The battles with the British in the two villages signaled the beginning of the Revolutionary War.

3

The Fighting Quaker

On April 19, 1775, the colonies went to war! Early that day, colonial militiamen engaged British troops in the small Massachusetts towns of Lexington and Concord. Men on horseback spread word of the fighting from town to town.

When the news of the battle reached Nathanael, he knew what he had to do. Saddling his horse, he kissed Kitty farewell and rode to East Greenwich to assemble with the other members of the Kentish Guards. At daybreak, the company left for Providence with the intention of going on to Massachusetts. But when the Kentish Guards reached Providence, the governor ordered them to return to their homes. Ignoring the governor, Nathanael and five others tried to continue their journey. But they reconsidered when they learned that the British troops had retreated to, and now occupied, the city of Boston.

Three days later, the Rhode Island Assembly met to select two commissioners to meet with the Connecticut Assembly. It wanted to determine the best way to defend the New England colonies. The assembly did not choose the two commanding officers of the Kentish Guards. Instead, much to everyone's surprise, it unanimously chose Nathanael as one of the men to represent the colony. At the same time, the assembly promoted him to the rank of brigadier general, in command of Rhode Island's army of 1,500 troops.

When Nathanael returned from Connecticut, he had little time to set his affairs in order. He asked his brothers to look after Kitty and prepared to assume his duties. The militia was to march to Cambridge, Massachusetts, to meet up with the militias from other New England colonies. Bringing together troops from various colonies, leaders had decided, was the only hope of opposing the British army. The next few weeks were hectic for Nathanael. Still, he always found time to write to Kitty. In one letter, he told her, "[I would have been] happy . . . if I could have lived a private life in peace and plenty. . . . But the injury done my country . . . calls me forth to defend our common rights and repel the bold invaders of the sons of freedom."

The 32-year old former Quaker disliked war but was anxious to see his first action. When he reached Cambridge, just outside Boston, Nathanael worked hard to prepare his troops for battle. Word quickly spread throughout the camp about the finely equipped and well-trained Rhode Island units. When General George Washington, commander of the Continental army, arrived in early July, it was Nathanael's **brigade** that was chosen as Washington's welcoming escort.

Soon afterward, the two men met. Nathanael

**George Washington meets with his officers.
He had great respect for Nathanael's
ability to make clever battle plans.**

was awed by Washington, and Washington
greeted Nathanael in a reserved but friendly
way. Though 10 years older than Nathanael,

Washington came to admire the younger man's skills as a military commander and **strategist**. Washington needed all the help he could get to keep his ragtag army in the field and ready to fight. Nathanael was important because he could not only guess the enemy's **maneuvers** ahead of time but also make a plan to defeat them.

Nathanael's love of mathematics may have helped him learn military strategy more quickly. His friend Henry Knox noted that Nathanael "came to us, the rawest, the most untutored being." But within one year, he was easily equal in military knowledge "to any General Officer in the army, and very superior to most of them."

Nathanael was the only American general, besides Washington, to fight the war from beginning to end. Like Washington, Nathanael believed that the colonies ought to fight as a whole, rather than as 13 separate armies. He later wrote, "I would as soon go to Virginia as stay here. The interests of one colony are in no ways incompatible with the interests of another."

Nathanael's military judgment was soon put to the test. At a council of war in Cambridge, Washington and his officers debated whether to attack Boston, which was now in the hands of the British. The British troops, or "redcoats" as they were known because of their bright red jackets, had strengthened their defenses around the city. It would be difficult for the Americans to break through. But some of Washington's advisors suggested they try anyway.

Nathanael disagreed, arguing that the British troops were probably weakening from lack of food and supplies. He suggested that Washington and his troops wait the British out; time was on the Americans' side. In the meantime, they could recruit additional soldiers, stock up on supplies, and continue preparing for combat.

Washington agreed with Nathanael. He knew that the Continental army was short of men, ammunition, cannons, and supplies. To attack Boston would be a risky undertaking at best, and would certainly cost more in lives than it was

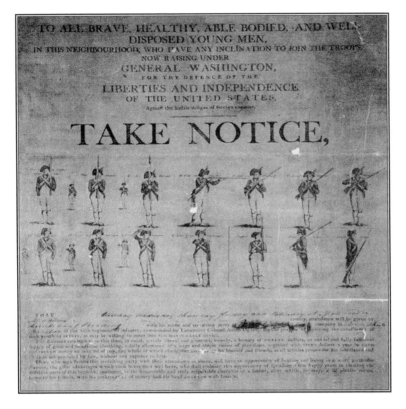

Nathanael advised George Washington not to attack Boston, but instead to recruit more soldiers with notices such as this one.

worth. And there was no guarantee that the American assault would free the city from British occupation. Washington put off the attack.

Nathanael received some welcome news from home. In Coventry, Kitty had given birth to their first child, a son. In honor of his commanding officer and friend, Nathanael asked that the boy be christened George Washington Greene. By late fall of 1775, Kitty and the child arrived in Cambridge to join Nathanael. For the next several months, the Greenes lived as a family.

In early 1776, Washington, who had grown tired of waiting, at last gave orders to break the Boston stalemate. Nathanael's old friend, Henry Knox, was now a major general and chief of artillery. On the night of March 2, 1776, Knox and his troops lugged 59 cannons through the bitter cold and snow and placed the artillery around the city of Boston. The next morning, the British commander, General William Howe, discovered American artillery trained on the British positions. Rather than face what was sure to be a disastrous battle, Howe chose to abandon the city. As Howe and his troops sailed out of Boston Harbor, General Nathanael Greene took control of the city for the Americans.

Later that spring, Nathanael went with the Continental army to New York City. Washington

Artillery commander Henry Knox and his men haul cannons from Fort Ticonderoga, New York, to Boston.

considered Nathanael one of his finest officers. When they reached Brooklyn, Washington put Nathanael in charge of the town's defenses and promoted him to the rank of major general.

But then Nathanael got sick with a high fever and was relieved of his command. During his recovery, he learned that the British had beaten the American troops at the Battle of Long Island. Knox was convinced that if Nathanael had been at the battle, "matters would have worn a very different appearance." Nathanael was not so sure. He later wrote: "I have not the vanity to think the event would have been otherwise had I been there."

Not yet recovered from his illness, Nathanael resumed his duties anyway. Washington placed him in charge of the troops guarding the New Jersey coast. From his headquarters at Fort Washington, on the rocky northern heights of Manhattan Island, Nathanael's command was to observe the movement of British ships.

Nathanael made a rare but terrible mistake. He allowed British ships to sail past the guns at the fort and take up positions on the Hudson River. The fort was now in danger, as was the entire Continental army. Washington was forced to move his troops further inland.

Nathanael refused to abandon Fort Washington. He believed that if the British attacked, his men could hold them off. Washington wanted to evacuate the fort immediately, but Nathanael persuaded Washington to be patient and give him a chance to correct his mistake.

British general Howe had other ideas. No doubt recalling his graceless exit from Boston, Howe ordered his troops to march on Fort Washington on November 15, 1776. He demanded that Nathanael surrender the fort immediately. Nathanael didn't back down. He ordered Colonel Robert Magaw to "stand fast." In the meantime, Nathanael and General Israel Putnam met with Washington at Fort Lee, New Jersey. Despite the British presence and Washington's concern, both men argued that Fort Washington was secure.

When they returned, Washington, Nathanael, and Putnam were stunned by the sight of Howe's troops attacking the fort. Although the Americans were outnumbered, Nathanael believed that the

British forces attack Fort Lee, across the Hudson River from Fort Washington. Both forts fell to the British in November 1776.

colonists would withstand the attack. Soon it got worse—the fort's outer defensive walls began to crumble. Despite Nathanael's pleas to stay behind and fight with his men, Washington ordered him to leave. Reluctantly, Nathanael obeyed. Washington's troops retreated to New Jersey, and eventually to Pennsylvania.

The fall of Fort Washington was costly for the

Americans. Nathanael felt horrible. In a letter to Knox, he lamented, "I feel mad . . . and sorry; Never did I need the consoling voice of a friend more than now."

Nathanael's reputation as a clever military leader was tarnished. Soldiers and officers alike began to question whether the man was really the "heaven-born genius" that Washington had called him. Even Washington was no longer certain about Nathanael. Nathanael viewed the event as an temporary setback. He vowed to exercise greater caution in the future.

He did not have to wait long for another chance. In the early morning hours of Christmas Day 1776, Nathanael helped to plan and execute a surprise attack on Hessian **mercenaries** encamped at Trenton, New Jersey. Leading his men in a victorious battle at Trenton went a long way to restoring his reputation. In January 1777, Nathanael again showed his courage at the Battle of Princeton.

Even in defeat, Nathanael proved himself a capable soldier. On September 11, 1777,

American troops clashed with the British at the Battle of Brandywine River in Pennsylvania. The British won that conflict, but Nathanael and his men held up the British advance long enough to allow the Americans to retreat without suffering the loss of additional men and valuable supplies.

Not more than a month later, Nathanael led the largest group of American troops ever assembled in the battle at Germantown, Pennsylvania. They were trying to capture the British troops camping nearby. Moving under the cover of darkness, Nathanael and his men lost their way in a thick fog and were 45 minutes late arriving at their appointed meeting place with Washington and his divisions. (So dense was the fog that British General Howe lost his dog. Washington recovered the pup and returned him to his owner under a flag of truce.)

The fog robbed the Americans of their advantage, and Washington wisely ordered a retreat. Although both Washington and Nathanael came under severe criticism for the defeat, Washington himself always believed that Nathanael's late arrival was not the cause of the American failure. Washington's confidence in Nathanael had been restored over time and he continued to regard his general highly. He even said that Nathanael should be the one to succeed him as commander in chief if he was captured or killed.

By 1778, Nathanael could add another title to his name. He was appointed the quartermaster general of the Continental army. Though Nathanael really preferred to be in the field, he graciously accepted the appointment out of respect for his friend Washington. The job was a very important one. The quartermaster general was in charge of obtaining supplies and money to feed, outfit, and equip the troops. It was also his duty to make sure that supplies reached the troops in a timely fashion. Nathanael tackled his new duties with the same determination he had given to his field command.

Still, he missed the fighting and asked to be

Nathanael's administrative skills were put to the test as the quartermaster general of the Continental army. The previous officer in charge had left behind a mess. Nathanael improved the transportation system by establishing a military supply line that reached throughout all the colonies. He stored equipment and food in cleverly hidden army depots. Working day and night, he had the department operating efficiently in just three months. Thanks to his efforts, the army could be easily moved, armed, and fed.

allowed to return to the command of his troops. For the moment, Washington refused. Nevertheless, Nathanael did see action in two important battles. In June 1779, Nathanael was once more at the head of his troops at the Battle of Monmouth, in New Jersey. Two months later, in August 1779, he proved himself in the fighting that took place at Newport, Rhode Island. As a measure of his confidence in Nathanael, Washington awarded him a command at Springfield, New Jersey, in the summer of 1780.

By this time, Nathanael had had enough of being quartermaster. In constant disagreement with Congress over how best to obtain supplies and funds, Nathanael threatened to resign his post and return to combat duty. Only the efforts of Washington convinced him to stay on until the army could locate a suitable replacement.

By this time, Washington had other worries besides finding a new quartermaster general. The British had won three major victories in the South by August 1780. The British now controlled South Carolina and Georgia, and there seemed to be little to stop them from sweeping through North Carolina and Virginia. The American patriots were discouraged. Washington needed a new commander to rally the Southern forces. But who could Washington call on to perform such an obviously important but seemingly hopeless task? Only one man came to mind.

Nathanael in his officer's uniform. In 1780, he became commander of the Southern army. Nathanael used brilliant strategies to defeat the British in the Southern campaign.

Second Only to Washington

I n October 1780, Nathanael received his new orders from Washington. "Congress having been pleased to authorize me to appoint an officer to take command of the Southern army . . . I have thought proper to choose you for this purpose. You will therefore, proceed without delay to the Southern army now in North Carolina, and take command accordingly." Nathanael could not believe he had been appointed commander of the Southern army, making him second in command to Washington. The post brought both opportunities and problems.

Nathanael knew the Southern army was in serious

trouble. British troops under General Charles Cornwallis had already defeated the Americans in Georgia and South Carolina. American troops were outnumbered, ill-equipped, and discouraged. If the British continued to move northward, North Carolina and Virginia would surely be captured. There would be no stopping the British from taking the rest of the colonies. The war would be over and the American quest for independence would be lost.

Nathanael wanted another opportunity to distinguish himself in battle. But he was also uneasy at the thought of being separated from his family. Kitty had often joined him when he campaigned with Washington in Pennsylvania and New York and while he served as quartermaster. By 1780, she and Nathanael were the parents of four children. The trips to see him were proving increasingly dangerous and tiring for Kitty and the children. So before he agreed to accept command, Nathanael asked to return home to make sure that everything was all right.

"I will prepare myself for the command as soon as I can," he wrote to Washington. "But as I have been five years and upwards in service . . . if it was possible I should be glad to spend a few days at home before I set out to the southward, especially as it is altogether uncertain how long my command may continue."

Washington was sympathetic to Nathanael's situation but could not spare him. He ordered Nathanael to report to him. Nathanael set aside his personal concerns and left immediately to meet with Washington in New Jersey. It was not only his family who missed Nathanael. The Continental army missed him as well.

After meeting with Washington, Nathanael went to Philadelphia to recruit more men and gather supplies. He made a point of surrounding himself with **seasoned** officers. He would need them, for when he arrived in Charlotte, North Carolina, Nathanael was shocked at the state of the Southern army. He had fewer than 2,000 ragged and starving men under his command–

men who looked more like scarecrows than sol-diers. Nathanael realized that before he could battle the British, he had to rebuild his forces.

But he did not have the luxury of time. The enemy would not wait for him to get his men into fighting shape. So he decided that the way to defeat the British in the South was to stage a series of surprise attacks. His small army would strike quickly and then escape before the British had a chance to strike back.

He unleashed small detachments under the commands of Francis Marion (known as "the Swamp Fox"), Henry "Light Horse Harry" Lee, and Daniel Morgan, with instructions to constantly harass the British army. Nathanael proposed to fight in a style unfamiliar in the 18th century. His Southern campaign would be a **guerrilla** war.

It was a daring, desperate, and dangerous strategy, but it worked. Nathanael's division of American forces into small, fast-moving units confused and exasperated Cornwallis. One of these units, under General Morgan's command,

**Nathanael's forces dealt an unexpected and
important blow to the British in 1781 at the
Battle of Cowpens.**

inflicted what Cornwallis himself admitted was
"a very unexpected and severe blow" at Cowpens in South Carolina on January 17, 1781.
After the Battle of Cowpens, Nathanael met with
Morgan to outline his plan to crush the British.
Morgan's troops were to join with other American forces at Salisbury, North Carolina.

Daniel Morgan had his doubts. He told Nathanael that he would not take responsibility should the operation fail. Nathanael replied calmly, "[I will] take the measure upon myself," realizing that "our prospects are gloomy notwithstanding these flashes of success."

Nathanael sent riders ahead to rouse the local militia, hoping it would keep the British busy long enough to allow Morgan and his men to reach Salisbury and cross the Yadkin River. The militia failed to respond, and another company of Virginians, whose period of enlistment had **expired**, left the army and returned home.

When he realized that reinforcements were not going to arrive, Nathanael could delay no longer. His plans had gone **awry**, so he set out for Salisbury in a heavy downpour, hoping to arrive there before the British and save Morgan's men from disaster. Muddy roads and swollen rivers slowed the British advance. When the British reached Salisbury, they discovered that the Americans had already fled north across the Yadkin River.

General Charles Cornwallis was the commander of all British troops in the South.

Cornwallis was furious. He brought up his artillery and ordered a barrage of cannon fire laid down on the American camp. A shell exploded near where Nathanael was preparing his report. As shingles and boards went flying, the unflappable Nathanael kept on writing. "His pen never rested," one of his staff officers recalled.

Now that his troops were reunited with Morgan's, Nathanael decided to regroup his forces at Guilford Court House, North Carolina, where additional troops supposedly awaited him. However, when he reached Guilford Court House, Nathanael saw that he had too few men to do battle. So he retreated northward, crossing into Virginia. Cornwallis was only too happy to follow, in the hope of trapping the Americans and forcing them to fight on his terms.

Nathanael guessed Cornwallis's intentions. To outwit his foe, he divided his forces and sent 700 men under the leadership of Colonel Otho H. Williams marching toward the Dan River, 70 miles to the north. Nathanael hoped to trick Cornwallis into following Williams, while he led the main body of the army eastward to safety. He told Williams to draw

Cornwallis deeper into Virginia and, at the same time, to turn his army slightly to the west. This westward movement would put even greater distance between Cornwallis's and Nathanael's troops.

Nathanael's plan worked. Cornwallis was completely fooled into thinking that he was in pursuit of the entire American force. He chased Williams for three days, all the while convinced that he was moving in for the kill. "I have him in my grasp," Cornwallis wrote with misguided delight.

The "Race to the Dan" was on, and Nathanael was determined to win it. In the process, he and his men suffered terribly. They trudged along dirt roads that the winter rains had turned into muddy soup. Hundreds were without boots or shoes. Many left bloody foot prints to mark the army's route. Despite these hardships, the plan was a success. Williams and his men helped the main army escape. When they learned that Nathanael and his troops had crossed the

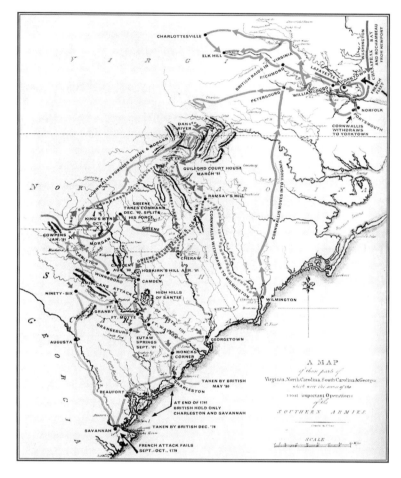

Army movements during the war in the South. Red lines show the routes of the American troops and green lines show the routes of the British forces.

Dan River and gotten away, the exhausted American decoys shouted with joy. Only then did General Cornwallis and his officers fully realize that they had been tricked.

The American troops had covered more than 200 miles, marching in wretched, wet, cold weather. Nathanael had not only gotten away from the British army but also forced Cornwallis to extend his lines of communication and supply beyond safe limits. The British had no choice but to return to North Carolina.

In late February 1781, Nathanael decided the time had come for the Americans to do more than carry out brilliant maneuvers and strategic retreats. Nathanael's army once more crossed the Dan River and set off to find the British, who only a short time before had dogged their very footsteps.

Continuously harassed by other American troops, Cornwallis slowly fell back. By mid-March, Nathanael's once pitifully small ranks had swelled to almost 4,200 men. The British, by contrast, found themselves for the first time terribly undermanned, with only 2,000 troops in any shape to fight.

Early in the morning of March 15, 1781, Nathanael, having recombined all his forces, moved to do battle at Guilford Court House. The fighting was bloody, and though it ended with the Americans withdrawing from the field, they inflicted such heavy casualties that Cornwallis at last decided to abandon the Carolina campaign. He retreated to Wilmington, North Carolina, then later moved north to conduct raids in Virginia, effectively surrendering control of North Carolina to the Americans.

Cornwallis had hoped that Nathanael would follow him to Virginia, where he thought his reinforced army stood a better chance of destroying the American troops and ending the war. Cornwallis

When he was not planning strategies with his officers, Nathanael was meeting with local officials or trying to find men and supplies. All in all, it made for long days. But, as his assistant recalled many years later, not all of Nathanael's time was devoted to work. Nathanael was known to have spirited discussions with his men about literature and mathematics whenever the occasion permitted.

Cornwallis Retreating !

PHILADELPHIA, April 7, 1781.

Extract of a Letter from Major-General *Greene*, dated
CAMP, at *Buffelo Creek*, *March* 23, 1781.

"ON the 16th Instant I wrote your Excellency, giving an
Account of an Action which happened atGuilfordCourt-
House the Day before. I was then perfuaded that notwithstanding we were obliged to give up the Ground, we had reaped the
Advantage of the Action. Circumstances since confirm me in
Opinion that the Enemy were too much gauled to improve
their Succefs. We lay at the Iron-Works three Days, preparing ourfelves for another Action, and expecting the Enemy to
advance : But of a fudden they took their Departure, leaving
behind them evident Marks of Diftrefs. All our wounded at
Guilford, which had fallen into their Hands, and 70 of their own,
too bad to move, were left at New-Garden. Moft of their Officers fuffered-- Lord Cornwallis had his Horfe fhot under him---
Col. Steward, of the Guards was killed. General O Hara and
Cols. Tarlton and Webfter, wounded. Only three Field-Officers
efcaped, if Reports, which feem to be authentic, can be relied
on.
    Our Army are in good Spirits, notwithftanding our Sufferings,
and are advancing towards the Enemy; they are retreating to
Crofs-Creek.
    In South-Carolina, Generals Sumpter and Marian have gained
feveral little Advantages. In one the Enemy loft 60 Men, who
had under their Care a large Quantity of Stores, which were
taken, but by an unfortunate Miftake were afterwards re taken.

Publifhed by Order,

CHARLES THOMSON, Secretary.

§†§ Printed at N. Willis's Office.

A letter from Nathanael announcing Cornwallis's retreat. Colonists posted copies of the letter in many cities.

was again disappointed. Instead of pursuing the
British into Virginia, Nathanael invaded South
Carolina and Georgia. In a series of important

battles, known collectively as the War of the Posts, Nathanael and his troops attacked a number of British fortifications. Three of these engagements in 1781–the Battle of Hobkirk's Hill in April, the Siege of Ninety-Six in May and June, and the Battle of Eutaw Springs in September–served to break the British stranglehold on the South.

Although none of these engagements was decisive in itself, taken together they substantially weakened the British war effort. By September, the British, who only a year earlier seemed destined to control the entire South, were now in control of only two seaports. When asked the secret of his success, Nathanael replied with disarming frankness, "We fight, get beat, rise, and fight again."

Nathanael never engineered a single **decisive** victory in the South; he did not need to do so. His old friend Henry Knox, among others, fully appreciated what he had accomplished. "The exalted talents of General Greene have been

Nathanael, astride a white horse, commands his army in an attack on the British at Eutaw Springs, South Carolina.

amply displayed in North and South Carolina," Knox wrote, "without an army, without Means, without anything he has performed wonders." There can be little question that Nathanael's superior strategy and leadership in the Southern campaign completely reversed the outcome of the American Revolutionary War.

The British surrender at Yorktown, Virginia, marked the end of the Revolutionary War. Afterward, Nathanael was surprised to be called a war hero.

"The Greatest Military Genius"

The war was finally over. General Cornwallis surrendered his army on October 19, 1781 at Yorktown, Virginia. But a year went by before Nathanael could make his way home to Coventry and to Kitty and their children. On his way north, Nathanael was surprised to be greeted everywhere as a military hero. All along his route, the locals honored him with speeches, testimonials, banquets, and celebrations.

His sudden fame made Nathanael very uncomfortable. When he could, he avoided crowds and preferred the company of friends and comrades. When he arrived at Trenton, he was delighted to find that Washington would accompany him as far as Princeton. There Congress was in session, and Nathanael was formally discharged from the army. As a token of appreciation from a grateful nation, Congress awarded Nathanael two British brass cannons that American forces had captured during the Southern campaign.

When he returned home to his family, which now lived in Newport, Rhode Island, Nathanael had little time to relax. He faced mounting financial problems. At the end of the war he found himself much poorer that he had been at the beginning. Private investments had turned out badly, and years earlier he had sold his interests in the family business to his brothers.

Nathanael's homecoming was very special. Not only was he reunited with Kitty; he could also, for the first time, be with all of his four children. He enjoyed visiting his many friends and was moved that his fellow Rhode Islanders had organized so many events to celebrate his accomplishments. None was more memorable than the ceremony held in East Greenwich where, almost 10 years before, Nathanael had nearly failed to gain membership in the local militia.

During the conflict, he had pledged his personal assets to pay for provisions.

Despite these setbacks, Nathanael and his family were far from broke. In gratitude for his service, the South Carolina **legislature** granted him 10,000 gold coins and a plantation called "Boone's Barony," located on the Edisto River. The Georgia legislature gave Nathanael an additional 5,000 gold coins and another plantation, "Mulberry Grove," situated on the Savannah River. Nathanael realized that these properties, if worked properly, could be very successful.

But there was another problem. Nathanael was against slavery. Yet, like other Southern planters, he had to rely on slave labor to make his plantations profitable. He found an acceptable compromise between his conscience and making money by granting his slaves the right to own a portion of the land they worked.

Nathanael and his family began making plans to move to Mulberry Grove. He sold Boone's Barony to cover some of his debts.

For the next few years, Nathanael traveled between Rhode Island and Georgia, taking care of financial matters. As with his past business ventures, he took an active interest in the daily operation of the plantation, often riding out to inspect the fields.

Eight years of military service had left Nathanael weary, and he was content to manage his plantation and spend time with his wife and children. He refused all requests to enter public life, twice declining to enter Washington's cabinet as secretary of war. He also turned down a county judgeship in Georgia.

But his reluctance to get involved in politics did not mean that Nathanael was uninterested in the life of the nation. Even in retirement he corresponded with Washington, Secretary of the Treasury Alexander Hamilton, governors, and other important statesmen. He offered his opinion on government and proposed solutions to the problems facing the United States.

In the fall of 1785, the Greenes moved to

After the war, Nathanael and his wife Kitty moved to the Mulberry Grove plantation, located along the Savannah River, in Georgia.

Mulberry Grove. Nathanael restored the house and gardens and planted new fruit trees in his orchards. He and Kitty soon became as popular in Georgia as they had been in Rhode Island. This period was among the happiest in Nathanael's life.

On June 12, 1786, Nathanael and Kitty went to Savannah to meet with some creditors. When they set out for home the following morning, the weather was already hot and humid. On the way back, they decided to stop at a neighbor's plantation so that Nathanael could inspect the rice fields. He spent several hours in the hot sun and, unlike his host, did not carry an umbrella to shield himself.

By the time they reached Mulberry Grove, Nathanael was complaining of a severe headache. The next morning he awoke in great pain, his forehead badly swollen. Kitty called a doctor, who examined Nathanael and then sent for another physician. It was too late. Early on the morning of June 19, 1786, Nathanael died at the age of 44.

A close friend who was at his bedside throughout his final illness later wrote, "I have seen a great and good man die." At the time, everyone assumed that Nathanael had died from sunstroke. Recently scholars have suggested that heart disease may have brought about his death.

Whatever the cause, Americans were stunned and griefstricken at the news. "Light Horse

Harry" Lee, one of Nathanael's former subordinates and a member of the Continental Congress from Virginia, lamented: "Universal grief reigns here. How hard is the fate of the United States to lose such a man. . . . But he is gone, and I am incapable of saying more."

Nathanael was one of the great leaders of the American War of Independence. Without his determination and genius, the British might have won the war. Nathanael's brilliance lay in his ability to quickly and correctly understand a military situation, guess his opponent's moves, and make the best plan of attack or defense. A master of strategic retreats, he could be very careful or bold and daring as needed.

During the Southern campaign, his actions saved the lives of the men in his army but also prevented the British from conquering the South. For his honesty, integrity, and devotion to duty, Nathanael won the respect and loyalty of his men and the admiration and friendship of his commanding officer. Placing him in the exclusive company of George Washington, his contemporaries regarded him as "the greatest military genius produced by the War for Independence." For many Americans, he remains so to this very day.

GLOSSARY

ancestors–a person's relatives who lived generations ago

astrologer–a person who predicts the future by looking at the stars and planets

awry–to go wrong

banish–to require to leave

bellows–a device that produces a strong blast of air used to feed a fire

brigade–a large body of troops

campaign–organized military operation

culprit–a person who has committed a crime

decisive–unquestionable, conclusive

descendants–offspring of a certain family or group

dilemma–any situation that requires a choice between unpleasant alternatives

entreat–request

expire–to end

forge–a furnace where metal is heated so it can be shaped into useful items

foundry–a place where metal is made for raw materials taken from the earth

grist–grain ready to be ground into flour

guerrilla warfare–small, quick attacks or ambushes against the enemy

husking bee–a gathering of people for the purpose of husking corn

legislature–a group of people given the power to make laws

maneuvers–planned and controlled movements of troops or warships

mercenaries–men who are paid to join a foreign army

militia–a group of civilian men called into the military only in emergencies

mother country–the country from which the people of a colony originally come

musket–a long-barreled gun

pacifist–a person who believes in peace and refuses to take part in a war

persecution–being punished for one's beliefs

Quaker–a religious group also known as the Society of Friends

seasoned–experienced

strategist–an expert in planning military battles

CHRONOLOGY

1742   Born on July 27 in Potowomut, Rhode Island, to a Quaker family.

1756   Enrolls in school.

1769   Father dies.

1770   Takes over operation of family foundry with brothers in Coventry.

1771   Serves as deputy to the Rhode Island General Assembly.

1772   British ship *Gaspée* is set on fire in Pawtucket, Rhode Island; Nathanael Greene is accused of leading the attack.

1774   Is banished from the Quaker community; marries Catherine "Kitty" Littlefield; joins the local militia, the Kentish Guards.

1775   Appointed brigadier general of Rhode Island militia; later appointed brigadier general in Continental army; meets George Washington.

1776   Promoted to rank of major general; commands a failed military action at Fort Washington on November 16.

1777   Leads troops at Battle of Brandywine and the Battle of Germantown, both in Pennsylvania.

1778   Accepts post from General Washington as quartermaster general of Continental army.

1780   Appointed commander of the Southern Continental army on October 14.

1781	Destroys one fourth of General Cornwallis's army at the Battle of Guilford Courthouse, in North Carolina, on March 15.
1783	Is discharged from military service.
1784	Retires to Mulberry Grove, Georgia.
1786	Dies on June 19; buried in Savannah, Georgia.

REVOLUTIONARY WAR TIME LINE

1765 The Stamp Act is passed by the British. Violent protests against it break out in the colonies.

1766 Britain ends the Stamp Act.

1767 Britain passes a law that taxes glass, painter's lead, paper, and tea in the colonies.

1770 Five colonists are killed by British soldiers in the Boston Massacre.

1773 People are angry about the taxes on tea. They throw boxes of tea from ships in Boston Harbor into the water. It ruins the tea. The event is called the Boston Tea Party.

1774 The British pass laws to punish Boston for the Boston Tea Party. They close Boston Harbor. Leaders in the colonies meet to plan a response to these actions.

1775 The Battles of Lexington and Concord begin the American Revolution.

1776 The Declaration of Independence is signed. France and Spain give money to help the Americans fight Britain. Nathan Hale is captured by the British. He is charged with being a spy and is executed.

1777 Leaders choose a flag for America. The American troops win some important battles over the British. General Washington and his troops spend a very cold, hungry winter in Valley Forge.

1778 France sends ships to help the Americans win the war. The British are forced to leave Philadelphia.

1779 French ships head back to France. The French support the Americans in other ways.

1780 Americans discover that Benedict Arnold is a traitor. He escapes to the British. Major battles take place in North and South Carolina.

1781 The British surrender at Yorktown.

1783 A peace treaty is signed in France. British troops leave New York.

1787 The U.S. Constitution is written. Delaware becomes the first state in the Union.

1789 George Washington becomes the first president. John Adams is vice president.

FURTHER READING

Alderman, Clifford Lindsey. *Retreat to Victory: The Life of Nathanael Greene.* Philadelphia: Chilton Books, 1967.

Bailey, Ralph Edgar. *Guns over the Carolinas: The Story of Nathanael Greene.* New York: William Morrow and Co., 1967.

Davis, Burke. *Heroes of the American Revolution.* New York: Random House, 1971.

Kent, Deborah. *The American Revolution: "Give Me Liberty or Give Me Death."* New York: Enslow Publishers, 1994.

Meltzer, Milton, ed. *The American Revolutionaries: A History in Their Own Words.* New York: HarperTorch, 1993.

Moore, Kay. *If You Lived at the Time of the American Revolution.* New York: Scholastic, 1998.

INDEX

PICTURE CREDITS

page

3: The Library of Congress
6: National Archives
10: New Millennium Images
13: The Library of Congress
16: The Library of Congress
19: The Library of Congress
21: National Archives
23: U.S. Naval Academy Museum
28: The Library of Congress
32: The Library of Congress
35: The Library of Congress
37: National Archives
40: U.S. Naval Academy Museum
46: National Archives
51: National Archives
53: The Library of Congress
56: The Library of Congress
59: The Library of Congress
61: National Archives
62: The Library of Congress
67: New Millennium Images

ABOUT THE AUTHOR

MEG GREENE earned a bachelor's degree in history at Lindenwood College in St. Charles, Missouri, and master's degrees from the University of Nebraska at Omaha and the University of Vermont. Ms. Greene is the author of five other books, writes regularly for *Cobblestone Magazine* and other publications, and serves as a contributing editor for Suite101.com's "History for Children." She makes her home in Virginia.

Senior Consulting Editor **ARTHUR M. SCHLESINGER, JR.** is the leading American historian of our time. He won the Pulitzer Prize for his book *The Age of Jackson* (1945), and again for *A Thousand Days* (1965). This chronicle of the Kennedy Administration also won a National Book Award. He has written many other books, including a multi-volume series, *The Age of Roosevelt.* Professor Schlesinger is the Albert Schweitzer Professor of the Humanities at the City University of New York, and has been involved in several other Chelsea House projects, including the COLONIAL LEADERS series of biographies on the most prominent figures of early American history.